THE
GHOSTLY TALES
OF
ROCKFORD

Published by Arcadia Children's Books
A Division of Arcadia Publishing
Charleston, SC
www.arcadiapublishing.com

Spooky America is a trademark of Arcadia Publishing, Inc.

First published 2024

Manufactured in the United States

ISBN 978-1-4671-9744-1

Library of Congress Control Number: 2023950130

Designed by Jessica Nevins

Images used courtesy of Shutterstock.com; p. 34 Rattis irrittis/Wikimedia Commons/ File:Tinker cottage.jpg/CC BY-SA 3.0; p. 52 Zissoudisctrucker/Wikimedia Commons/ CC BY-SA 4.0; p. 64 Eddie J. Rodriquez/Shutterstock.com; p. 106 Tracy Immordino/ Shutterstock.com.

Notice: The information in this book is true and complete to the best of our knowledge. It is offered without guarantee on the part of the author or Arcadia Publishing. The author and Arcadia Publishing disclaim all liability in connection with the use of this book.

Spooky America

THE GHOSTLY TALES OF ROCKFORD

SELENA FRAGASSI

Adapted from Haunted Rockford, Illinois by Kathi Kresol

arcadia
CHILDREN'S BOOKS

TABLE OF CONTENTS & MAP KEY

OHIO

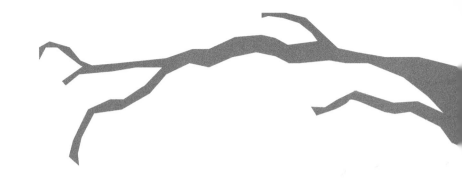

Welcome to Spooky Rockford!

Tucked away in the northwest corner of Illinois, just a ninety-minute drive from Chicago, is the quaint and charming town of Rockford. Most famously known as the home of the Rockford Peaches from the beloved 1992 baseball movie, *A League of Their Own*, Rockford is a sporty, outdoorsy, and family-friendly city. Though it's not as big as Chicago, nearly one hundred and fifty thousand residents presently call Rockford home.

Rockford even has its own airport, which means a lot of people, especially business travelers, like to come here. So, it's not surprising that Rockford has earned the nickname, "Illinois's Second City."

But it's not all business in Rockford. The scenic Rock River dazzles visitors every year with its miles and miles of bike trails along the waterfront and activities like paddling, wakeboarding, canoeing, and kayaking. Known as "The City of Gardens," Rockford is also home to some of the most beautiful Japanese gardens in America. In fact, with its natural beauty, outdoor attractions, and laidback lifestyle, it's no wonder *Life* magazine

once hailed Rockford as "... typical of the U.S. as any city can be."

But do you know what is *not* so typical? All the ghosts that are running wild across Rockford!

Now, you may be skeptical of the paranormal. You might even think it's impossible for ghosts to be real! But after reading these truly chilling tales, it's possible you'll get some goosebumps and change your mind. You might even decide to visit Rockford some day to see with your own eyes what others swear they have witnessed.

Part of the reason Rockford might be so haunted is because it contains three core elements that almost *guarantee* a visit from the great beyond. First, Rockford sits along the Rock River, and bodies of water are known to channel spirit energy. Second, it has limestone, a powerful mineral that allows poltergeists (a type of mischievous ghost) to cling to the energy and become stronger. Finally, Rockford is home to many burial grounds that once belonged to the Indigenous peoples of North America.

Just one of these elements could make a town haunted—but all three? That's like *asking* for your town to be haunted, and just too creepy!

With all those spooky elements combined, it's no wonder Rockford is such a ghostly hotspot! From a number of *very* haunted houses—including one called the Demon House, where a woman was said to have become possessed by a dark spirit—to bony skeletal figures lurking in water fountains, these totally creepy ghost stories will test the notion that Rockford is simply a "quaint" Illinois town.

So much for being typical, right? Now, read on, if you dare, and find out for yourself what you *really* believe about the supernatural.

The Ghost of Geraldine Bourbon

When *Haunted Rockford, Illinois* author, Kathi Kresol, and her children moved into a giant old farmhouse in Rockford's quaint School Street neighborhood in 1988, they didn't expect the very strange things that started happening. From the moment the moving vans drove away, and the family began to unpack, something felt very off. Sure, the beautiful home had a big yard with crisp green grass, and plenty of bedrooms for all four of the children to sleep and play. But despite its charm, all was not what it seemed inside this old, mysterious farmhouse.

Late at night, Kathi and her family sensed the feeling of a dark cloud hanging over them as they slept. Many times, when the family would go to bed—anticipating dreams of field trips or upcoming vacations—the TV in the family room downstairs would suddenly turn on, even though no one was anywhere near it. Night after night, deafening sounds of TV static would blare through the house without warning, rattling everyone upstairs from their slumber.

It only got worse from there.

Many objects around the house would go missing, and then turn up in strange or unexpected places. Baby bottles for Kathi's youngest daughter once mysteriously disappeared from her crib, only to be found months later *inside the walls* when the family started on some renovations to the home. At first, Kathi thought maybe it was her children playing tricks on her—they were all under the age of five and very mischievous, after all. Then again, they couldn't possibly have hid baby bottles inside a wall!

Nonetheless, Kathi kept finding strange things in her home—like the "possessed" paper towel holder in the kitchen. Any time a roll ran out and she replaced it, the new roll would suddenly start to spin, unravelling all by itself into heaps on the floor!

Other times, lights would flicker on and off even when there wasn't a storm—or any other logical reason for glitchy electricity. If that wasn't bad enough, Kathi and her family always felt as if they were being watched, like a pair of eyes were following their every move.

Even the pets knew something was not right! The family's dogs and cats constantly looked up at the farmhouse's ceiling as though something were hovering above. In one terrible instance, one of the family's pups mysteriously got locked inside a room. It howled with fright until Kathi discovered the trapped dog. When she let it out of the room, the poor thing ran away faster than it ever had in its entire life.

Eventually, Kathi decided she needed to figure out what may have happened inside her house. Maybe then she'd be able to solve the mystery behind all of the strange occurrences. Many families had lived in the house since it was built in 1913, so there was a lot of history to start researching. Kathi had heard rumblings from her neighbors about a terrible tragedy that had happened at the farmhouse in 1958. Kathi was very curious, so she went to the local library to see what she could find out. After looking through old newspapers from 1958, Kathi finally came across the story of a murder that made her skin crawl in panic!

There, on the very front page of the newspaper dated January 18, 1958, was a vintage photo of Kathi's house with the headline, "Geraldine Bourbon, murdered on School Street." Kathi was so shocked, she let out a yelp that caused people in the library to give her the stink eye! But none of that mattered to Kathi now. She grabbed the newspaper and rushed into a corner where she could read for herself what had happened to Geraldine.

Kathi learned that Geraldine had been married to a man named Laurence. He was her second husband. Her first marriage happened when she was very young and still living in Wisconsin, where she was born in 1929. Geraldine had two children with her first husband, but when they divorced, the kids stayed with their father while Geraldine moved to Rockford to start a new life.

In 1951, at the young age of twenty-one, she met and married Laurence Ray Bourbon after they dated for just a short time. Laurence was in the army, which meant the very adventurous Geraldine could travel to her heart's desire while following her husband in his years of active service. That brought them all the way to Germany in 1957, where they lived and raised their two young children. But it wasn't exactly a happy time.

Laurence had awful bouts of depression and drank too much. After a series of mishaps, he was discharged from the army. The family packed up their home in Germany and moved to Rockford, Illinois. The Midwest town was near both of their families (Geraldine's in Wisconsin and Laurence's in St. Louis, Missouri). Eventually, Laurence found his footing again, got a good job in construction, and the family was able to move into a cozy apartment. But sadly, Laurence's mental health struggles and drinking continued, making Geraldine unhappy, and even fearful of what he might do to her or the children.

In early January 1958, Geraldine confided to her sister Arline that she was scared of Laurence and wanted to leave him. A couple of weeks later, she got the courage to do so. She packed up her belongings and necessary items for her two children, and fled with them in the middle of the night while Laurence slept. They went to live with Arline and her husband William in their beautiful old farmhouse on—you guessed it—School Street. The *same* house that Kathi and her family now

lived in, and the place where Geraldine's fate was unfortunately sealed on January 18, 1958.

Laurence was none too happy that Geraldine had left him and their family broken. He knew she was living with Arline on School Street, and on that cold, mid-January morning, he headed to the house to try to get her back. Laurence found the door unlocked, so he barreled in carrying a gun and began making threats. Arline ran to the mechanic shop next door and begged the men inside to help her. The shop owner stopped the work he was doing in his office and grabbed the phone to call the police.

But it was too late.

As Arline raced back to the house to get the children to safety, shots rang out. *Multiple* shots. When the police were finally able to get into the School Street house, they found both Geraldine and Laurence dead in an upstairs bedroom. Laurence had shot Geraldine, then turned the gun on himself and fired.

As soon as Kathi finished reading the newspaper article, she decided to call a realtor to sell her house and move her family. She finally understood that the heaviness they'd all felt inside the house—and the many spooky occurrences they'd witnessed—were no doubt the work of Laurence and Geraldine, whose restless spirits were still lingering inside the old farmhouse. Though Kathi felt sorry for their tragedy, she was happy to leave Laurence and Geraldine behind and let them settle their differences in the afterlife.

CHAPTER 2

The House Emma Jones Won't Leave

A beautiful home sits near the Rock River on Rockford's east side. It has stunning curved windows and a protruding tower that goes up to the third floor, making it look like a mini-Midwestern castle. But no one wants to live there. Why? Because Emma Jones still *does*—even though she's been dead for years!

While she was alive, Emma was very happy living in her lavish home. She had a loving marriage to her husband Frank (they wed in 1898), and they had two successful sons, Ray and Carl. As he got older, Ray helped Frank run the family's trucking business. Both Ray and Frank were often gone on business travel, but Emma kept herself busy. She had two dogs she doted on like her other children, and she always found things to do around the house, whether tending to her garden or simply sitting in her third-story attic, watching the boats coast along the river below.

But as time passed, and everyone grew older, the situation inevitably changed. One morning in December 1941, as Emma got out of bed to let the dogs out and make breakfast, she noticed that Frank was not waking up. Emma pushed him, called his name, and reminded him he was going to be late for work—but he didn't move. Sadly, Emma soon found that Frank had passed away peacefully in the middle of the night.

Emma was simply heartbroken. She cried every night when she went to bed, hoping the night would take her, too. As sad as she was, Emma remained in the house with her two dogs, dreaming of the days when everything was perfect, and Frank was still alive.

Ray died not too long after, and so did Emma's beloved dogs. After so much loss and sadness, Emma's health started to decline, and she began experiencing dementia (a condition that impairs a person's brain function and can cause memory loss). Her son, Carl, felt it was no longer safe for Emma to live in that big old house all by herself. So, he had his mom come live with him a few blocks away. But that didn't stop Emma from finding her way back home, sometimes in the middle of the night.

Neighbors would see her standing in the driveway, just staring for hours at the beautiful old house that was once hers. Concerned for Emma's well-being, they'd call Carl so he could tend to her.

"I'll be right there," he'd tell them, and he'd drive over to comfort his mom and bring her back to his house. But night after night, Emma kept sneaking out to "go home," and Carl decided it was time to sell the old family property and put an end to her confusion for good. Carl hired a young and eager new realtor who knew he had a gem on his hands. The empty house was a marvel of beauty— except, it wasn't empty anymore. Not by anything *living*, of course.

One day, while preparing to show the home to potential buyers, the realtor discovered the lights weren't turning on, so he went to the basement to reset the fuse box. He was having trouble finding his way in the dark, so he lit a match. As soon as he held it up to help guide him, the realtor had the scare of his life. He saw an old lady standing right in front of him with a smile on her face! Just then, the lights came back on, and the woman was gone.

For a moment, the realtor just stood there, scared out of his wits. Had he really seen the old lady, or were his eyes playing tricks on him? He took a deep, shaky breath and reminded himself: *there's no such thing as ghosts.* Then he headed back upstairs, as if everything was fine. That was a big mistake! Because, as it turned out, the very first couple he showed the property to instantly fell in love with the home and decided to buy it.

But . . . they didn't stay for long!

Soon after the couple moved in, they experienced very strange sensations that kept them up at night. A loud knocking would come from nowhere, echoing all around the house. Sometimes, they'd even hear what sounded like dog collars jingling and dog claws scraping the floorboards—even though they had no pets.

The final straw came one night when they were about to sit down in their living room to watch some TV. Only, instead of watching their favorite movie, they watched an old lady suddenly appear in the corner, asking them why they were in *her* house.

Let's just say that the couple wasn't expecting to watch a horror movie that night!

The couple ran out of the room, locked themselves in a bathroom, and phoned a neighbor. "Oh, that's just Emma," the neighbor said, telling them about the old lady who would get confused and wander back to the house. "Just call the family."

The neighbor gave them the family's phone number, but when the couple dialed it, they were shocked by what they learned: Emma had died three weeks earlier.

That was all the couple needed to hear, and they immediately moved out.

The next unlucky man to buy the house stayed for even less time than the couple before. He also heard the strange knocking and metal dog collars clanging. But even more disturbing was that every night when he'd try to fall asleep, his phone would ring. On the other line was always an old lady asking, "Am I dead?"

Can you even imagine the nightmares he had?

If you're ever in Rockford and drive past Emma's house, look closely at the upstairs attic. Chances are, you'll see her gazing out the window, phantom dogs by her side, dreaming of days gone by.

By Demons
Be Driven

Have you ever thought about *Stranger Things* really happening in our world? It may sound crazy to think that kids could fight off demons trying to destroy all of humankind just by traveling through secret portals. But let us give you a real-life example, and then it may not sound so far-fetched after all! If you talk to Vaughn and Sheri who lived on Rockford's east side in the 1980s, they'll tell you all about the *strange things* that happened in their home—known to many around town as the Demon House—which they swear was no fantasy in the least.

The couple and their five children moved into their beautiful home in 1981, they but only stayed for one year. They frantically left in the middle of the night to escape the constant terror that was happening day after day.

It all started innocently enough. They thought the footsteps they heard climbing up from the basement stairs were just old, creaky floorboards giving way. The TV that always turned on by itself in the living room? It probably just needed to be replaced. And the pots, pans, and dinnerware that kept disappearing? That *obviously* had to be the

kids' friends playing around and forgetting to take the items back to the kitchen . . . *right*?

Not so much, as it turned out. Soon, things started getting weirder, scarier, and more difficult to explain. Once, Sherri was walking across her living room when, right before her eyes, a small ceramic trinket that sat on her piano split in two, as if sliced by an invisible blade!

Soon, the children became too scared to go to sleep, because every night, their beds would shake with such a powerful force, it would nearly throw them to the ground! The family noticed terrible, awful smells coming from the basement, and meanwhile, there were no longer just footsteps coming up the stairs. Now, it sounded as if someone—*or something*—was trying to jiggle the doorknob to break loose into the rest of the house!

The mystery ghoul in the basement got so aggressive that one day, when Sherri was having coffee with a friend in the kitchen, they suddenly heard very loud growling—like that of a large beast—from behind the basement door. Terrified it would break free, Sherri and her friend rushed to secure the door. Sherri put all her body weight into the door to keep the beast at bay while her friend grabbed a chair to block it from opening. As Sherri leaned into the door with all her might, she felt a stark chill come over her body. It scared her so much, she and the friend ran to a neighbor's house and called the police. The officers investigated, but when they observed the kitchen and basement, they found nothing. Even Sherri struggled to explain what had happened.

Another really odd thing? The number of the case file as noted on the police report ended in 666, which many believe is the mark of the Devil.

With the police unable to help, and not sure where to turn next, Sherri and Vaughn recruited a local ghost hunter in Rockford. He tried to channel the spirit and talk to it during a séance in the house. A séance is at type of ritual performed where the participants attempt to contact the dead. Except, this séance went terribly wrong, and the gruesome being possessed Sherri instead! Her face started morphing into an animal-like creature, her eyes got wide and changed color, and all of a sudden, she let out a huge growl that sounded nothing like her!

Thankfully, as quickly as it had began, it was over. Sherri came out of her possessed state but had no idea what happened, though Vaughn and the ghost hunter pointed out scratches all over her body. The ghost hunter told them, "This is not a ghost you have here; this is a demon." He suggested they leave the house immediately, but Sherri and Vaughn had one more idea.

They contacted a priest from a Rockford church to see if he'd perform an exorcism—an old religious ritual with the purpose of casting a demon out of a possessed human being. Today, exorcisms are rare, and religious scholars doubt their validity. But the priest said he would do it, only insisting that Sherri and the couple's five children not be in the home for their own safety. With everyone in agreement, Vaughn, the priest, and the ghost hunter stayed behind, and the three men began the exorcism.

They focused on the basement, since that's where it seemed the demon spirit was living. Later, in an article written in the *Rockford Register Star*, all three men reported an intense cold coming from wherever the spirit would linger just below. For nearly two hours, the men recited prayers, sprinkled holy water everywhere, and demanded the spirit leave the house immediately.

Eventually, it felt like a huge weight had been lifted from house, and the men hoped the demon had been cast from the basement. Sherri and the kids soon returned home, but the priest could not be fully certain the family was safe or that the demon wouldn't return.

With enough terrible nightmares to disturb their sleep for a lifetime, Sherri, Vaughn, and their children soon moved away, and were never heard from again. They had already beat the demon back once, but not without the beast instilling a permanent fear deep in their bones. If there was ever a next time, they might not be so lucky. So, who could blame them for leaving Rockford and never looking back?

Ghost Hunting at Tinker Swiss Cottage

There is one house in all of Rockford that is so haunted, it's even been featured on the TV show *Ghost Hunters*. During the episode, a team of paranormal researchers went inside to figure out exactly who—or *what*—was lurking in the shadows and causing so many scares. What they found was so creepy, this place could only be described as a house of death!

The house is called the Tinker Swiss Cottage, but don't let the cozy name fool you—there's nothing cozy about this place! Today, it's a historic house museum and park that guests can visit when they come to town. On the outside, the cottage still has its beautiful European charm. There's a large, upside-down V roof, wooden balconies, and lots of intricate carvings that make it look like a chalet you might find at a ski resort. The lush gardens and winding paths let you take in the beauty as you walk the grounds.

Back in the early 1900s, the cottage belonged to the Tinker family. Robert and Mary lived there for much of their lives. They met when Robert came to work for Mary's business, the Manny Reaper Company. It was originally owned by John Pels Manny, who built the also-haunted Manny Mansion. But more about *that* in due time, fearless readers.

John's business associate was Mary's first husband, and when he died, he left the entire company to her. Though Mary and Robert had no children of their own, guests often crashed at the home for a night ... or a month ... or even a year at a time.

But the one thing they all had in common? All of them died inside!

One by one, every visitor took their last breath on a bed inside the home until there was no one left to spare. You'd think the guests would take a hint!

First, it was Mary's dad Josephus, then Mary's niece Marcia, and finally Mary herself. All of them were found dead in their beds within a few years.

Not only did they all die in the home, they had their funerals inside, too, which was a common practice during those times.

The extra creepy part, though? To this day, most of their belongings are still in the house! Everything from the couches they sat on, to the clothing they wore—even their personal diaries where they spilled all their secrets.

If that isn't spooky enough, the Tinker Swiss Cottage also sits on land across from an old cemetery full of scattered, crumbling headstones. Even weirder, it's perched on a limestone hill overlooking a body of water called Kent Creek.

If you get where we're going with this—BINGO! Water and limestone are big signs that a place could be haunted. And Tinker Swiss Cottage is *full* of signs.

Anytime a ghost hunting team goes into the cottage, they experience unexplained occurrences that put a real chill in their bones, leaving some running out the front door. These are paranormal professionals and even *they* are scared! Regular visitors can take ghost tours through the cottage, too, but let's just say the tours have a . . . *reputation*.

Once, as a group was wrapping up their time inside, a guest flagged down the hosts to tell them how much she'd loved the event and learning about the Tinkers. She'd especially loved that they'd hired actors dressed up in old-fashioned clothes and retro hairstyles to really make it feel like it was the early 1900s.

"We don't have any actors, and no one dresses like that," the host told the woman. Suddenly, her face turned pale and white, just like she had seen a ghost. Likely because she *had* just seen one!

Another time, the ghost tour group was walking through different rooms upstairs in the Tinker Swiss Cottage when everyone heard a woman's voice from downstairs call out very loudly, "*Hello?*"

Thinking that someone had come late to the tour, one of the hosts went down the staircase to meet the woman and bring her to join the group. Except...there was no one there. Just then, he remembered the doors were locked, having secured them himself only thirty minutes earlier. The host went from room to room—the living room parlor, the kitchen, the bathroom—looking for the lost person. But no one could be found anywhere. When he rejoined the group, he asked, "You all heard that voice, right?" And everyone shook their heads very slowly as they realized what they'd heard was not human at all.

It seems that Robert Tinker really doesn't like all these guests coming in and out of his home, and he might be playing tricks them. Once, when a ghost hunter was in the basement of the cottage, he turned on his cell phone's recorder feature to hear what voices might come through. And, sure enough, loud and clear came a man's voice, blaring through the phone.

"Get out!"

The ghost hunter did not hesitate to do so!

Other times, when the Tinkers are ready for people to leave, they make it pretty obvious. Doors will slam shut, or items will go flying right at the guests—as if thrown by an invisible hand! They're small things like pennies and coins, nothing that would hurt anyone. But still, it certainly gets the message across.

Other paranormal phenomena continue to give people the creeps when they're in the cottage. Some visitors report feeling bony hands on their shoulders, even when no one is around. Other guests have heard the voices of children laughing and playing (just one problem—children aren't allowed on the ghost tours!). Others, still, have seen full-bodied ghosts living and breathing right next to them. A popular ghost is a frantic maid who runs up and down the staircase while trying to bring the Tinker family their dinner.

One ghost tour brave enough to visit the Tinker Cottage on Halloween got an extra dose of spooky tricks and treats. The group was peering into the bedrooms on the second floor when, suddenly, the lights went out and the whole house became pitch black. While everyone gasped at the sudden change, one woman let out a bloodcurdling scream and started crying. When the lights came back on,

she said she felt someone's hand running down her back ever so slowly ... but no one had been standing next to her. The woman immediately ran for her car and sped away, never to return.

This is certainly becoming a theme in Rockford, right? Should we continue and learn what other terrors await us in this so-called "*typical town*"?

We thought you'd say yes—so here we go!

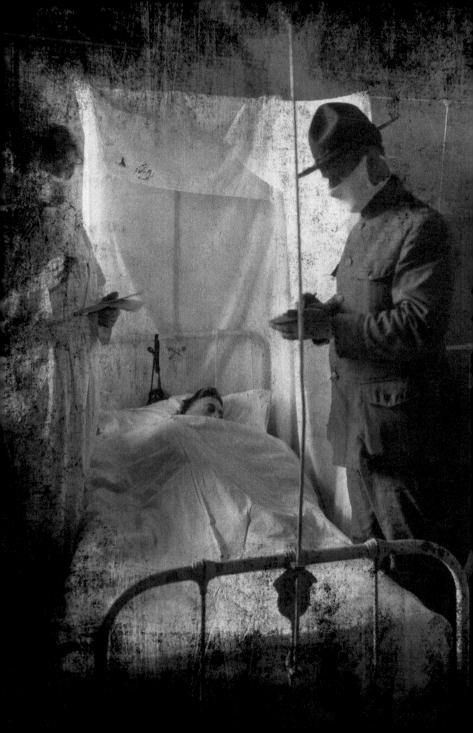

CHAPTER 5

The Tragedy at Camp Grant

During World War I and II, Rockford was the site of a very important—and *very* haunted—military base called Camp Grant. Built in 1917, it was where men and women preparing to go off to the battlelines were housed, fed, and trained before being deployed overseas.

Camp Grant had a massive spread of eleven hundred buildings that served fifty thousand people at one time. It was so big that it was recognized as its own town, with its own fire department, hospital, and movie theater. It's amazing to think about how many soldiers passed through here—and, sadly, how many soldiers were never able to return.

One of them was the very respected army colonel Charles B. Hagadorn. He came to Camp Grant in 1918 to help run the massive military base during World War I. The timing was terrible, though. The very contagious Spanish Flu was spreading like crazy throughout the United States and had devastating effects as many people became sick and died. Just think back to how devastating COVID-19 has been in recent years and you'll know how early Americans felt back then; perhaps even worse because they didn't have the benefits of modern medicine as we do today.

Millions of people across the world died due to the Spanish Flu, hundreds of thousands of them in the United States alone. In fact, Rockford became one of the worst places for infection, as the flu spread rapidly among the thousands of soldiers who lived and worked at Camp Grant. They were in such close contact at the site, often sharing bunkers. It's as if the flu placed a bullseye on the soldiers' backs. The first case was reported on September 23, 1918. Within three days, seven hundred people were sick. Within a month, that number jumped to a devastating four thousand people.

This would be stressful enough for anyone to witness, but Colonel Hagadorn was devastated and fearful. He didn't know what to do as he saw more and more bodies pile up at Camp Grant every single day, like a huge mountain of death, unable to stop the carnage.

The military man had long suffered from insomnia, which

is when a person has a problem falling and staying asleep, and it became even worse for Colonel Hagadorn during this time. He couldn't sleep a wink throughout the entire pandemic, as his mind wandered with anxious thoughts and feelings of helplessness.

However, the ghosts of dead soldiers could have been keeping him up at night. He would pace the halls, talking to himself at all hours of the night. One night, he was overheard crying out in pain, "My God . . . these deaths are appalling!"

The lack of sleep and deep depression were wearing on him, until finally, on October 8, 1918, Hagadorn was found dead in his bed. It appeared

the Colonel had used one of his military weapons to end his own life.

Decades later, Camp Grant would become the Camp Grant Museum and Command Post Restaurant, where visitors could sit down for a meal after exploring the historic grounds. Though both closed in 2020, visitors remember plenty of spooky happenings. Some said they'd strangely lose their appetite by the time they reached the restaurant. That's because many reported sensing, or even *seeing*, the ghost of good ol' Colonel Hagadorn, himself! Perhaps his restless spirit left an uneasy feeling in the pit of guests' stomachs?

Some who claim to have seen his ghost describe Colonel Hagadorn as looking like he just stepped out of one of his photos hanging on the walls! A waitress who worked the restaurant remembers getting ready to open for lunch one afternoon when, out of the corner of her eye, she noticed a figure in full soldier's garb. But as she turned her head to get a closer look, he vanished into thin air!

Objects were also known to strangely move around from time to time, like the place settings, silverware, and saltshakers on restaurant tables. Camp Grant's former owner, Yolanda, thought it might be the Colonel (or another spirit) trying to get her attention.

You see, Hagadorn isn't the *only* ghost lingering around the grounds. Many of the previous employees claim to have seen shadowy figures of men and women in aprons that darted through the restaurant as soon as they were spotted. Yolanda

once saw one of these bizarre spirits once for herself: He laughed at her as he raced through the venue! Yolanda called his bluff and followed his path, but the ghost's voice kept trailing off as he got farther away. He ultimately vanished before she could catch him. Another time, Yolanda felt a hand tap her shoulder, but when she turned around, no one was there!

It eventually became such a frequent occurrence, Yolanda would tell the ghosts good night when packing up at the end of each day. All she'd ask is that they not come home with her since, after all, she'd just see them tomorrow. And anyway, it's not healthy to take your work home with you!

CHAPTER 6

Evenings in the Burpee Museum

Have you ever visited a museum and wondered if any of the artifacts and exhibits come alive at night, after everyone leaves? Do woolly mammoths and dinosaurs start roaming the halls? Do campfires crackle as prehistoric families cook dinner, just as they did tens of thousands of years ago? If the thought has ever crossed your mind, you probably don't want to get locked inside any of the buildings belonging to Rockford's Burpee Museum of Natural History!

Spread out over multiple buildings on Main Street, including two former mansions, there is something peculiar happening at the Burpee Museum. Specifically, the section once known as the Barnes Mansion is also known for its frequent hauntings. Whether it's the life-like taxidermized animals (taxidermy is a way of preserving an animal's body after it dies for study or display) and preserved bugs inside the glass cases—or simply just phantoms lurking around corners—*something* trapped at the Burpee Museum loves attention!

Back in 1953, a man named William Fletcher Barnes built the mansion for his family, and he, his wife, and their children lived there together for many years. Today, it's still as gorgeous as it was the day it was completed. There are fifteen rooms and many circular windows, plus balconies and turrets that make it look like a real castle! William was a very rich man who put a lot of his money into the home. He and his brothers had a successful company making woodworking machines that were very much in demand at the time and sold all over the world. Because he worked with these machines, William was able to make all the beautiful molding, archways, and fireplace mantels inside the mansion—all obvious places ghosts can hide! It was so stunning, many believed it was the most beautiful home in all of Rockford.

Decades later, the Rockford Park District bought the Barnes Mansion. They turned the first two floors of the home into the Burpee Museum in 1942, while the relics and fossils moved to a larger building next door. Today, the mansion remains as offices for many employees who work for the museum, and most of them report very strange activity, especially when they leave work and lock up for the night. So much so that no one wants to be the last one out!

Sometimes, after turning off the lights in the mansion for the day and getting into their cars

The GHOSTLY TALES OF ROCKFORD

to head home, the employees will see the lights turn back on as they drive away. Other times, loud classical music will suddenly start to play, almost like there's a symphony concert in the house! But with only a few people left in the building, and hardly a musical instrument in sight, there's no *way* all that noise is being made by the living.

It all happened when an employee, Susie, was working late one night in her office on the first floor of the mansion. As she was getting ready to pack up to go home, she heard what sounded like vintage swing music coming from a radio in an upstairs room—even though it was the 2000s and swing music was rarely played on the radio. Susie thought maybe her coworker, Alex, had turned it

on, perhaps to listen to while working late answering emails. She decided to check in on him and see if he wanted a ride home. Except, when she got to the top of the stairs, she found his office dark. No lights on, and no Alex!

Now, most people would have taken that as a sign to run away, but not Susie. She approached the office door and cracked it open. As soon as she did, the music stopped, and a large chill swept over her body. It felt like someone had passed by her even though there was not another soul in the mansion. Well, no *living* soul, that is!

Susie immediately flew down the stairs and out the front door—it's a wonder she ever came back to work again!

The Barnes Mansion is unique in many ways: it was built near the Rock River and, as we mentioned before, water can be a major super-highway for supernatural energy. It's also near Rockford's beautiful Beattie Park, which sits on old Native American burial mounds.

As hauntings typically go, if there are bodies in the ground, there's some paranormal activity around town!

But the most likely reason for the hauntings are the many tragedies the Barnes family experienced while living in the mansion—including the many deaths. It was as if the family was cursed! Could their spirits be trapped inside? Could their sorrow be preventing them from moving from this world to the next? That may be *precisely* what has happened.

William Barnes and his beautiful wife Julia had four children: Katherine, Aimee, Joseph, and William Fletcher, junior (they called him W.F.). When the children grew up, Joseph entered the family woodworking business, and W.F. became a race car driver. Katherine and Aimee married and had families of their own. While most parents will never admit to having a favorite, it was clear Joseph was the apple of William Barnes's eye.

Imagine his sadness when, in 1905, Joseph died tragically due to a terrible disease called typhoid. But guess where his funeral was? Inside the mansion!

Yes, his body was laid at rest for a full day in the parlor as people came inside and paid their respects. Not only that, but Joseph's cold corpse was left in the basement for days prior, while the funeral director prepared it for the services. Some say, even though Joseph's body was later buried, that his spirit never left the Barnes Mansion. To this day, Burpee Museum employees do not like going down into the basement. Not only do they feel like they are being watched, but many have also experienced a very heavy sadness suddenly come over them, as if they need to cry for reasons that can't be explained.

But that was not the only tragedy for the Barnes family. In 1910, Joseph's son—Joseph Jr.— also died suddenly. Shockingly, the young boy's widowed mother, Adeline, had just married her second husband not twenty-four hours before the seven-year-old passed away.

As Adeline and her new husband departed for their honeymoon, Joseph Jr. went to stay with his aunt, who took him and his cousin for a trip to downtown Rockford. They were told to wait for her in the car, but Joseph Jr. didn't listen. He opened the car door and exited to play in the street. Almost immediately, he was hit by an oncoming vehicle and killed.

Sadly, tragedy continued for the Barnes family through the decades that followed. Matriarch Julia suffered a gunshot wound while on a family hunting trip just across the border in Wisconsin. Several bullets hit her face and exited an eyeball. She miraculously survived but lived the rest of her days with a lot of pain. What's odd is that some believe Julia knew who shot her...but would never tell anyone who it was.

What secret do you think she was keeping?

Whatever happened that day, Julia took it to her grave. And though she passed away in 1922, many people say they still see her ghostly figure and disfigured face in an upstairs window, gazing out as if frozen in time.

Another historic home in Rockford, the Manny Mansion, also belongs to the Burpee Museum of

Natural History. Constructed of limestone, it's located along the waterways of the Rock River, near Beattie Park, making it prime real estate for the paranormal! The stunning structure is complete with a large wraparound porch, regal columns, and dozens of arched windows, perfect for growing lots of spiderwebs. And, like the Barnes Mansion, it appears to be haunted!

For some time, it belonged to a New Yorker, John Pels Manny, and his family—the same John Manny you read about earlier. They, too, endured many tragedies; so many that their story reads like a movie script.

John Manny and his wife Eunice had five lovable children, but they were sadly never able to grow up. All but one of them, the oldest boy George, suffered horrible fates and died tragically young. After the baby, Katie, passed in 1867, it's said Eunice was so heartbroken, she died soon after. Perhaps all she wanted was to somehow be reunited with her children.

John remarried and miraculously had five *more* children with better fortune, but they couldn't escape death completely. Their baby girl, Lucretia, died at the age of one. Can you imagine all that death in one family? Overcome with so much grief, John built a towering monument at Rockford's Greenwood Cemetery to honor all of his family who had passed. He would go here often and "visit" them. In fact, it was here at this very spot in the graveyard where he sealed his own fate. One day while visiting the family plot, John was thirsty and took a drink of water from a fountain. But it was contaminated, and soon he contracted typhoid and died himself.

The Manny mansion was eventually taken over by the artist and funeral undertaker, Harry Burpee, whose name inspired the Burpee Museum. At first, he wanted to use the building as a funeral parlor, but neighbors didn't like that idea—the house seemed haunted enough! So, it became an art gallery, and then a location within the Burpee Museum.

Should you enter the Manny Mansion today, you may experience oddities similar to what the staff have reported over the years, like hearing old-fashioned music when no one is around to play it, or lights going haywire for no reason. But be warned: the spirits here are not happy about all the changes to the mansion. Paranormal researchers once picked up voices from the beyond, all saying how much they *disliked* the ways their home has been remodeled ...

It must be true what's often said: Everyone is a critic, even ghosts!

The Show Goes On at the Coronado Theatre

Illinois is far from Hollywood, California, but over the years, plenty of movie stars and singers have loved to come to Rockford to take the stage at the Coronado Theatre. People from all over town put on their best tuxes and furs for a night out to see shows starring people like funny guy Bob Hope, the famous actor and tap dancer Sammy Davis Jr., and Hollywood actress Bela Lugosi (star of the super creepy *Dracula*). Even John F. Kennedy took the stage at the Coronado once when he was campaigning to be president!

Today, you might go there to see Disney's *Encanto* or spend an evening with *Star Trek* legend William Shatner. But those who have tickets often get more entertainment than they bargained for, thanks to a cast of ghosts that pop up at any time, causing a lot of drama!

Most of the time, it's just Willard and Erma Van Matre. The lovely old couple were the first owners of the building. They loved it so much, they lived there for a large part of their lives—and seem to never have left! Willard and Erma were both born in Chicago in the late 1880s and moved to Rockford with their families when they were very young.

They met and married in 1911 but were separated for a few years when Willard was stationed in France, serving the United States during World War I.

Upon returning home, he decided his life's mission would be to open a theater, but not *any* average theater. He wanted to create one that made people feel like they were sitting outside under the stars, watching their favorite movies, comics, and music performances. (In the dark is where the best horror stories happen, too!)

Willard used lights to make it look like the sun was rising and setting inside, played music that sounded like birds chirping, and even had a starry ceiling built with flickering lights. It looked like the

Milky Way was dancing magically over everyone's heads. Willard's idea was very unique to Rockford, and people from everywhere came to see it.

The Coronado Theater opened in 1927 and was a big hit from the beginning. It was so successful that Willard and Erma bought out several more theaters in town and had a booming business. But their hearts always belonged to the Coronado, where they even lived upstairs for what seemed like forever (and may end up having been just so!).

They were great hosts and often went downstairs for the events. Willard would dress up in his finest tuxedo and shake the hands of people entering through the doors. And, despite having died in 1953, he apparently continues to do so! Many people have reported feeling his bony skeleton hand touch theirs when they least expected it.

How fast would you pull away your hand if that happened to you? Me? *Fast*.

But even though Willard and Erma have been

gone for more than fifty years, they haven't really disappeared, and apparently a good number of ghost friends have joined them. Because if you have to spend eternity somewhere, you can do much worse than this beautiful place. How could you honestly fault them?

You can bet ghosts are around when you start to smell cigar smoke and whiffs of perfume, even though no one is allowed to smoke inside anymore, and there's no one around that could possibly be doused in so much perfume! Strange voices are sometimes heard near empty seats, and even full-body ghosts have been spotted—like Willard in his tux! When big shows are happening, he still likes to come watch them and greet guests. There's even a rumor that if you stare at the large mirrors in the main lobby long enough, you might just see Willard appear right next to you!

Step inside Willard and Erma's old apartment, and it's even spookier. There is a grand old cabinet that holds little trinkets Erma collected over the years. It was her favorite piece of furniture, and apparently still is. If you touch the cabinet or stand near it for too long, you'll soon feel a blast of cold air shoot down your spine. Could it be a draft from an open window? Or might it be a warning sign from the beyond to leave the cabinet alone? Be warned, those who don't listen may really make Erma mad.

But it's not just Willard and Erma who are haunting the Coronado. A mystery "woman in white" is frequently spotted as well. One of the theater's current employees was locking up the building one night when he suddenly had the strange sense he was being watched. Though he couldn't see anyone as he walked around the theater, he decided to get out his camera and take a few snaps just in case. Sure enough, in the pictures, a ghostly woman in a white dress appeared. When the worker zoomed in, he could see her so clearly, he even noticed her hair hung in a loose bun. His hands started shaking, and he nearly broke his camera as it felt to the floor.

This unknown lady has been reported many times over the years. In 2014, police were called to the Coronado to investigate. They focused on the elevator in the theater's parking garage across the street. Someone said that a person kept riding the elevator up and down, up and down, never getting off or letting people on. It was getting annoying, as they needed to get back to their cars so they could go home!

When police arrived on the scene, they were as confused as everyone else. As they watched the elevator glide up and down, they stood in wonder

as they observed no one inside. Later on, police were able to get a vague description from one witness who said they saw a woman in a white dress. But no one was *truly* certain of what they saw—and how it could possibly be.

Some locals think it could be the restless spirit of a young mother who died inside the theater long ago. Her baby was playing a small role in a play, and she was backstage caring for him between acts. Sadly, out of nowhere, she collapsed on the floor and died immediately. Thankfully, a man was standing next to her at the time. He caught the baby as it fell from her arms, preventing two lives

from being lost that day. Perhaps the mysterious woman in white is the ghost of the young mother, eternally searching for her long-lost child?

If you should visit the Coronado, try to arrive around Willard and Erma's anniversary, or Erma's birthday—you might just catch a glimpse of a ghost couple waltzing across the stage in their finest Sunday best to the sounds of a phantom orchestra. But don't worry, they always save a dance for their beloved guests!

Lost Love Inside the Veterans Memorial Hall

Has your mother ever told you that her love for you will never die? It's one of those corny things moms like to say, meaning they'll love you even when you're not together. But for some parents, like Della Damon, they really mean it!

The Rockford native and her son, Grant Damon, have both been dead for a long time, but sadly, they never got to say a proper goodbye. So, now, they are spending all of eternity haunting the same building in Rockford while trying to reach each other. And in the process, they're sending very mixed messages to the many humans with whom their spirits come in contact!

For nearly one hundred years, the Damons have been haunting Rockford's Veterans Memorial Hall, which opened in 1903. It's known as the first in Illinois—and possibly in all of America—to honor the men and women of the armed forces. The Memorial Hall was so important that President Theodore Roosevelt came all the way from Washington, D.C., for the grand opening.

But of course, the Memorial Hall's history is also full of spooky stories!

Some think the Memorial Hall could be haunted by Army Commander Thomas G. Lawler, the military man who pushed for the Memorial Hall to be built in the first place. In fact, Lawler loved it so much, he even had his funeral inside the building! That's right, his cold, lifeless corpse lay there for more than four hours as hundreds of people from

Rockford and beyond paid their respects. That's quite a long time to let a spirit explore and find some good hiding places!

The other thing that's unique about Rockford Veterans Memorial Hall is that it's filled with uniforms, medals, and certificates from many generations of veterans' families that fought in the World Wars and the Vietnam conflict. Many of those brave men and women are now dead, but their spirits could still be clinging to these mementoes of which they were so proud. Some visitors have heard heavy footsteps in the Memorial Hall, like military boots marching the floor, while others have heard the faint sound of trumpet salutes playing, just like you might hear at a soldier's funeral.

But the best-known ghost story at Veterans Memorial Hall is that of Della and Grant Damon. So many times through the years, people have seen a woman roaming the building. She's always wearing a long gown and moves very slowly. Some have seen her walking, possibly even *floating*, down the main staircase. Others have noticed the phantom lady going into different rooms, as if she's looking for something she lost.

One time, the ghost took on such a human form that a visitor mistook her for a living person. The visitor was locked outside of the Memorial Hall and waiting on the sidewalk when she happened to see a woman inside through a window. The visitor knocked on the glass, hoping to catch the woman's attention so that she might unlock the door. But even as the visitor's knocking turned to pounding, the woman never turned around—or even flinched. It's like she hadn't heard a sound!

The woman walked away toward the basement, completely out of sight. Later, when the visitor finally got back inside the building, she shared her story with the manager. But he was confused. All day long, he explained, there hadn't been anybody inside the Memorial Hall ... except him.

It's most likely the ghost of Della Damon, who

continues to look in every corner for her son, Grant. He was a soldier shipped off to France in 1918 to fight for the United States during World War I. During the Christmas season of that year, he was finally coming home for a visit. Della was so excited to see her boy that she decorated the family home with a Christmas tree and hung stockings. She even bought a roast to cook. When all was ready for Grant's arrival, Della went to the Veterans Memorial Hall in Rockford to get more details about when his train would arrive at the station.

But tragically, the only thing waiting for Della there was an envelope, and the notice inside shared news she couldn't possibly have been prepared to hear.

"We regret to inform you that your son has been killed."

Della nearly collapsed on the cold marble floor when she read those horrible words.

She would dine alone that Christmas season, but what did it matter? Her son was dead.

Today, Della's eternal sadness still hangs heavy in the air of the building. In fact, if you sit on one of the benches in Veterans Memorial Hall, a very strange sensation will come over you. All of a sudden, you'll feel incredibly sad, even if you were just laughing and joking seconds before! Could it be the same bench that broke Della's fall? We'll never know, but it certainly seems plausible.

Perhaps surprisingly, the spirit of Grant Damon is also lurking around the Memorial Hall. Ghost researchers were able to communicate with him one time using EVP, a tool ghost hunters use to communicate with paranormal entities, and Grant told the story of how he died.

While fighting for the U.S. Army, Grant and his battalion were hit with poisonous mustard gas. He was wearing a gas mask, but when Grant saw a fellow soldier who had been wounded in the battle and didn't have a mask on, he rushed over to help.

Grant took off his face shield and put it on the soldier, helping to carry him away to safety. Sadly, the fellow soldier never made it. Worse still, Grant became very sick from the effects of the mustard gas, and he passed away, too.

Della had only learned of Grant's death when she went to the Veterans Memorial Hall to reunite and rejoice with her beloved son. But as the years have gone by, the pair have remained ghosts unto themselves, carrying all the sorrow and heartbreak of a mother-son reunion that has never come to be.

CHAPTER 9

The Unwanted Dinner Guests

When you eat at one of Rockford's many restaurants, you can expect tasty food—and maybe even a scare or two! One notorious place is Lucerne's Fondue and Spirits. Inside the colorful yellow and purple building, the "spirits" on the menu don't just refer to the cocktails being served. Ghosts might also pull up a chair and join you!

There's one time the owner, Mark, remembers very clearly. It was Valentine's Day night, a very popular holiday for Lucerne's since its cozy, romantic vibe is perfect for couples. Every seat in the house was full for Cupid's holiday. Lovey-dovey guests were dipping meats and cheeses in melted fondue. Waiters dodged one another as they carried trays full of food and drinks. And there was a lot of loud chatter in the background as people carried on lively conversations.

Mark turned on some music—Frank Sinatra—to help set the romantic mood. But as Frank crooned his famous song, "The Way You Look Tonight," a strange evil suddenly emerged from the speakers, such a mean and terrifying voice that it brought the entire dining room to a screeching halt. Diners stared at one another in fear for a split second before a voice screamed, "Get out . . . get out *now*!"

Everyone in the restaurant suddenly dropped their silverware, frozen in panic and confusion. Even one of the waitresses immediately took off her apron and handed it to Mark, quitting her job on the spot.

Early another day, Mark arrived at Lucerne's to get some paperwork done. But as he walked inside the restaurant, he immediately felt something was off. It was summer and the air conditioning was on full blast, but the restaurant felt very hot, like a bunch of people were inside, creating body heat.

Mark checked the kitchen and the bathrooms—no one was there. But then, something else caught his eye. He looked down and realized that the phone system's green light was on—a light that only came on when someone was using the phone. Mark's heart began to pound. Who could be on that line? He was the only one in the restaurant.

Wasn't he?

Now Mark was pretty frightened, even more so when he quickly headed up the staircase to his office on the second floor and felt a cold chill come over him. Mark yelled out a warning to anyone who may have been inside: "I'm coming up!" The moment he said it, the lights instantly went out and Mark knew for sure he was not alone.

Pulse racing, he sped back downstairs and out the front door, promising himself he'd only ever do paperwork at Lucerne's again when other people—as in *living* people—were around.

One must understand Lucerne's is a very old building, with lots of characters who once lived there. It was first constructed in 1895 for Olin Brouse and his wife Lillian. They were married in 1891 and had two children, Charles and Florence. Lillian was a beautiful young woman who had a lovely singing voice and was well-known in town. Olin was considerably older than her and became sick a few years after they moved into the house. Lillian found an in-home caretaker who made Olin comfortable until he died.

Some people, like Mark, believe it's the couple and the health aide whose spirits are still trapped inside Lucerne's. Maybe Lillian doesn't like when Frank Sinatra sings, so she raises her voice, warning people to get out. Maybe it's *Olin* who likes to move tables and chairs around. Or just maybe, it's the caretaker whose phantom footsteps can be heard at random times on the staircase. Whoever it is, Mark often reminds the ghosts of his one and only rule: they can have the run of the house when Lucerne's is closed, but just don't scare off the patrons.

Der Rathskeller Restaurant is another *super*-haunted spot in Rockford. Its name alone sounds daunting, doesn't it? The German food spot was first opened in the 1930s by an immigrant named Fred Goetz. He lived at Camp Grant while enrolled in the military, and he loved the city. Except, he had a heck of a time trying to find the German sausages he loved to eat.

He started driving across state lines into Wisconsin to get his hands on his favorite food, and before Fred knew it, he was buying sausages for friends, too—up to eight hundred orders at one time! As you might have sensed, Fred knew this could end up being a lucrative business, and so he opened Der Rathskeller.

Fred's wife, Irma, helped run the restaurant until she sadly died in January 1947. Irma was in a car with the couple's daughter, Lucy, who was behind the wheel. Suddenly, Lucy hit an icy spot in the road, lost control of the vehicle, and slammed into a semi-truck. Both women were thrown from the car. Irma died instantly. Lucy survived but needed a lot of care, which was provided by an in-home nurse, Bertha. Can you even imagine the guilt Lucy felt?

At least something good came out of the sad situation. Fred fell in love with Bertha, they married, and she helped manage Der Rathskeller. All three of them—Fred, Irma, and Bertha—loved the dining venue so much, it appears they never really left.

Thankfully, their hauntings are pretty playful. Fred loves messing with the napkins—after waitstaff roll them into their nice, fancy design for the restaurant tables, Fred gets to work unrolling them, making the waiters have to start all over again. As you can imagine, this gets really old after a while!

However, one of the current owners of the restaurant, Mike, has had some more frightening experiences. Late at night when he is all alone, he sees spooky shadows out of the corner of his eye and has even heard his name called out!

It might be Irma—she's pretty vocal. Ghost researchers have recorded her on their EVP machines saying, "Where are my cabinets?" They've also felt the cold sensation of her ghost roaming around the dining room, moving objects around. Clearly, she still has incredibly high standards and is not pleased Der Rathskeller doesn't look exactly the way she had it all those years ago ...

Regardless of who owns the eatery, it seems as though Irma is still the boss!

The Ghoul of Haskell Park

There was once something in the water fountain at Haskell Park—something that mysteriously only came out at night, when innocent and unaware people were walking by. It slowly emerged from underneath the surface of the crystal-clear water, taking on a dark black shape as it grew and grew even taller than the fountain itself! The elusive creature had bony hands, just like a skeleton, and without warning, those hands would reach right out and grab you! And if you tried to run, it would run after you!

Clearly, this was no Casper the Friendly Ghost haunting Haskell Park. It wasn't there to play little games on the living. No, this dark spirit was mad and disturbed and would go after *anyone*—man, woman, child, dog—who dared cross its path.

The beast that haunted the fountain was first spotted in 1902. That's when a man shared his story with the local Rockford newspapers of his near kidnapping by the wretched ghoul. He'd been walking through Haskell Park late one night, around midnight, when he thought he'd heard a strange sound as he neared the center of the park, right where the majestic fountain once stood. The way the bright moonlight was hitting the fountain illuminated the water. It drew the man in, making him stop to take a closer look as he wondered what could be making all the ruckus.

Then, right before his very eyes, a dark and shadowy figure started to rise out of the misty water. It wasn't totally clear at first what it was. Were his eyes playing tricks on him? Could the water just have been making a wave? To the man's horror, the dark blob began to take on a human shape. But it was bigger than a human; it was like Bigfoot come to life! Except, instead of being covered in fur, *this* ghost's defining trait was that it had super thin, bone-exposed hands—just like a rotted-out corpse.

It was like nothing the man had ever seen, and before he could even pause to think, the skeletal hands reached out to grab him. The man ran through Haskell Park, screaming for his life. He ran all the way home and immediately locked the door behind him, his heart still racing in his chest.

This wasn't the only time the water demon was spotted. Over the years, many Rockford residents reported encounters with what appeared to be the Devil himself coming out of the fountain in Haskell Park.

Even in more recent years, though the fountain is now long gone, it's been said this spirit, so determined to capture humans, has chased people all the way to the edge of the park! It's only here, near the gates to the outside world, that the frightened few were able to finally break free from its grip.

It has become such a well-known ghost story in Rockford, in fact, that people often avoid walking

through Haskell Park after dark. Wouldn't you try to find another park to walk through, too? Even so, some still dare to enter the park at night and have said they can see the dark shadow hiding in the trees nearby ...

No one knows for sure who the malevolent spirit is or why he's so angry, but nonetheless, its evil has lived for decades, lingering in Haskell Park and waiting to claim its next human trophy.

CHAPTER 11

Spooky Happenings on Bloods Point Road

Resilient readers, you have come this far, proving you're at least open to the idea of the spirit world. But let's cut to the chase: Would you drive down a road called Bloods Point?!

NO WAY! The name alone would make most people stay away. Even so, wouldn't you at least be curious how it got its name?

We thought so.

The long and winding stretch of road just

outside Rockford continues to be a very popular haunted attraction. Many ghost hunters and the paranormal curious head here to see if it's really a portal to the underworld. As they get in their cars and drive at night, they wait for something to jump out of the shadows. And, boy, do they ever get the scare of their lives!

As they drive the forty-miles-per-hour speed limit and look out the widows, they likely spot long-hanging tree branches that sway in the wind, appearing to point at the drivers to turn around and go home! Things get even spookier when the moonlight shines brightly on the hood of the car and morphs into an evil eye, glaring like it wants them to leave!

Then, suddenly, the ghost hunters will hear an ear-piercing sound of metal scraping the road. Without warning, a big black dog will appear, wearing a large metal choker collar. The dog's terrifying, growling face will appear in the window, barking its head off, showing big fangs dripping with drool. Its nails will hit the glass trying to get in! It makes absolutely no sense—where did the dog come from and how did it catch up to a vehicle going *forty* miles per hour? Yet, in Rockford, it happens all the time.

So does the large, ghostly pickup truck that will drive too close and ride people's car bumpers. The truck's headlights are so bright, they nearly blind everyone in the car and almost cause a collision. When the victim speeds up, so will the pickup truck—a scary car race that seems to have no end. Until, suddenly, the pickup disappears, just as if it melted into the pavement.

Or vanished into thin air.

Some say the ghost dogs and truck are phantom guards of the cemetery, which stands on Bloods Point Road. But others think it could be something far more sinister.

There are many wild stories about Bloods Point that have existed in local folklore for decades. While the name sounds cryptic, it's actually in honor of a real man, Arthur Blood, who was one of the first to settle in the Rockford area. He is also one of the characters in an old urban legend—one about Beulah the Witch.

Beulah was a very mean old woman who hated children. She was a neighbor of Arthur Blood, his wife, and their brood of kids who lived on a large farm just outside Rockford. The Bloods were kind folk, though, and didn't believe the stories about Beulah. She was actually quite nice to them and played with the children when the parents were away. At least, until the terrible winter of 1842, a season that produced some of the worst snowstorms in Rockford history. It killed crops and much of the livestock in the area, leading people to go hungry and lose their homes. When spring came, so did wildfires, further devastating the town of Rockford.

Many of the residents assumed Beulah had cast a spell on the town, and that she alone was responsible for Rockford's tragic circumstances. It certainly felt like a curse. But in their ignorance, and though she denied any wrongdoing, the townspeople hunted after Beulah, anyway. They chased Beulah from her home near the Blood family and forced her into the woods, leaving her stranded and defenseless.

To get her revenge, it's said that Beulah lured

all the town's children—including the Bloods—to her forest cabin where she kept them for eternity, never to return to their families. Today, some people driving down Bloods Point Road say they see an old lady holding a cat in the middle of the street. Once they get close enough, the cat will jump out of her arms and run toward the car, almost causing them to crash. It's a trick Beulah uses to kidnap more victims!

Beulah the Witch, also known as the Witch of McGregor Road, is a ghost story that has existed in Rockford for many, many years. But was she real? Well, that depends on what you're willing to believe. There once lived a woman named Beulah Andrews who had a very creepy past. In 1913,

local newspapers reported that police were called to a family farm outside Rockford, after a horrible fight broke out and one of the daughters was attacked with a hammer. It was Beulah. Many in her family had been suffering terrible headaches and illnesses and said they were sometimes forced to dance uncontrollably. They believed Beulah was a witch and casting spells on them—and they'd had enough. They figured the only way they could make the spells stop was by killing her. In fact, the only person who took Beulah's side in the whole thing was her father.

After the horrible fight in the home, all of the family were put in jail and made to stand trial in front of a judge. Beulah swore she didn't practice witchcraft and her father stood up for her. The judge told the family they would be split up. Beulah would live with her father back on the farm, while her mother and other siblings would move away to live with a relative. Some say Beulah was so heartbroken being away from her mother and sisters that she turned into a mean, old witch looking for revenge.

Others believe the story of Beulah goes back to a teacher who taught in a school near Bloods Point.

She loved her students, but one day, the building caught fire and killed several of the children. Beulah was devastated. She tried everything to save the kids. But the parents never forgave her. It's said that the torment this poor woman received over the accident drove her insane, leading her to wander the woods where she would call out the names of the children who died in the flames.

Many stories have changed over the years as people pass the legend of Beulah down to new generations. The legend of her luring children to her home in the woods has led many teenagers to try and find her cabin late at night. Some will drive by and beep their horns, or even throw gifts at what they believe is her home, just to try to get Beulah to open the door and reveal herself. And many times, she does!

A Ghostly Goodbye

Now that you've heard tales of demonic possession, fatal tragedy, and merciless witches, goblins, and ghouls that hide in plain sight in the allegedly "typical" Rockford, Illinois, are you starting to believe in the supernatural?

Of course, what may be true and what may be fantasy is entirely up to you to decide. But should you ever find yourself in Rockford, be sure to stay alert and keep an eye out at all times. Because whether it's an odd breeze, or a cold bony skeleton hand waiting to take you in its grips, nothing is ever just a coincidence in Rockford.

Or perhaps we should really say...nothing is *ever* typical.

Selena Fragassi is a Chicago-based writer who grew up in a real haunted house. She has loved all things paranormal since she had her first experience with a ghost as a teenager. In addition to writing for the *Spooky America* series, Selena is a music journalist and, among other titles, has written books on New Kids on the Block. She has contributed to publications such as the *Chicago Sun-Times*, *A.V. Club*, *Blurt*, *Paste*, *Popmatters*, *Under The Radar*, and *Nylon*, among others. Selena is working on an upcoming novel about her grandfathers' experiences during World War II. You can follow her on Instagram or X (formerly Twitter) at: @SelenaFragassi.

Check out some of the other Spooky America titles available now!

Spooky America was adapted from the creeptastic *Haunted America* series for adults. *Haunted America* explores historical haunts in cities and regions across America. Here's more from the original *Haunted Rockford, Illinois* author, Kathi Kresol:

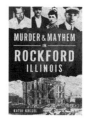